The Gift of S[...]

A teaching document of the Bishops' Conferences
of England and Wales, and of Scotland

Catholic Bishops' Conference of England & Wales

Catholic Bishops' Conference of Scotland

The Gift of Scripture

Catholic Bishops' Conferences of England and Wales, and of Scotland

Published by The Catholic Truth Society.

The Catholic Truth Society
40-46 Harleyford Road
London
SE11 5AY
www.cts-online.org.uk

Copyright © 2005 Catholic Bishops' Conference of England and Wales and Catholic Bishops' Conference of Scotland.

Published as a teaching document of the Bishop's Conferences of England, Wales and Scotland, approved for publication by decree of the Congregation of Bishops, Prot No. 134/2005 dated the 6th day July 2005.

All rights reserved. No part of this publication may be reproduced or stored or transmitted by any means or in any form, electronic or mechanical, including photocopying, recording, or any information storage and retrieval system, without prior written permission from the publisher.

Biblical quotations are taken from the New Revised Standard Version. A more literal rendering has sometimes been provided in order to illustrate particular points.

The cover shows the icon *Christ the Redeemer, Source of Life,* c. 1393-94 (tempera on panel) by Byzantine, Skopje, Macedonia © Lauros/Giraudon. Folio from St John's Gospel, facsimile of *Codex Sinaiticus*, 4th century AD, © Clarendon Press, Oxford / Bible Society, London, UK.

ISBN 1 86082 323 8

contents

Foreword 7

Introduction 9

    1. A book for today 9
    2. The Scriptures in these lands. 9
    3. An ancient tradition 10
    4. Word and Sacrament 11
    5. Scripture and the Church 11
    6. The layout of the document 12
    7. At your word, Lord! 12

Part One: Hearing the word of God

He sends out his word to the earth. (Psalm 147:15)

    8. God's loving initiative 13
    9. The Son, the fulness of all revelation. 13
    10. Scripture and Tradition 14
    11. A living Tradition. 15
    12. The role of the Magisterium 16

Part Two: Understanding the word of God

Was there ever a word so great? (Deuteronomy 4:32)

    13. God's word in human language 17
    14. The truth of Scripture 17
    15. The inspiration of Scripture 18
    16. A parallel with the Incarnation 18
    17. The human dimensions of Scripture 19
    18. The unity of Scripture 20
    19. The danger of fundamentalism. 20
    20. The dynamism of Scripture 21
    21. The Fathers of the Church 21
    22. The rule of faith 22
    23. A balanced approach 22

Part Three: Reading the Old Testament

Your words became to me a joy and the delight of my heart.
(Jeremiah 15:16)

24. An immense collection 23
25. The canon. 23
26. The deuterocanonical books 24
27. The Old Testament 24
28. In the beginning 25
29. A chosen people. 25
30. The exodus and the covenant 26
31. Laws of life 26
32. The promised land 27
33. The kingship 28
34. The prophets of Israel. 29
35. The suffering of the prophets 29
36. Prophecy and fulfilment 30
37. The Wisdom literature 30
38. The problem of suffering 31
39. The Psalms 31
40. Apocalyptic visions 32
41. God's patient teaching 32

Part Four: Reading the New Testament

The word of the Lord endures for ever. That word is the good news which was announced to you. (1 Peter 1:25)

42. The climax of revelation 34
43. The four gospels 34
44. A unique literary genre 35
45. The good news of the kingdom of God 36
46. Mark's story of Jesus. 37
47. The suffering Messiah 37
48. The death and resurrection of Jesus 38
49. Matthew's opening chapters. 38
50. The Sermon on the Mount 38
51. Jews and Christians in Matthew 39
52. Matthew and the Church 39

53. Luke's stories of the birth of Jesus. 40
54. The good news to the poor 40
55. The ministry of Jesus to women and their ministry to him. 41
56. To seek out and to save the lost 41
57. Did not our hearts burn within us?. 42
58. The Fourth Gospel 42
59. The signs in John's gospel. 43
60. Jesus' farewell words 43
61. John's portrayal of the death of Jesus 44
62. The Risen Lord 44
63. The apostolic preaching 45
64. The journeys of Paul 45
65. Paul's mission and gospel 46
66. Pastoral problems of the pauline churches 46
67. Christ and the Church 47
68. The other letters 48
69. The Book of Revelation. 48

Part Five: Living the word of God

The word of God is still at work in you who believe. (*1 Thessalonians* 2:13)

70. The enduring relevance of the Scriptures 50
71. A rapidly changing society 51
72. The new evangelisation 51
73. Scripture and catechesis 52
74. Scripture and the liturgy 53
75. Honouring the word. 53
76. The role of the reader. 54
77. The homily 54
78. Other Liturgies of the Word 55
79. The Liturgy of the Hours. 56
80. Bible reading for all. 56
81. Biblical formation and resources 57
82. Our debt to other Christians and to the Jewish people 57
83. Common witness to the word of God 58
84. Our final prayer 58

Documents. 60

Foreword

'You will be my witnesses to the ends of the earth.' (*Acts* 1:8) The Lord's words to his disciples have echoed across the centuries. They are addressed to us today.

We are in the early years of a new millennium. The world in which we are called to be Christ's witnesses has much in common with the world in which the apostles began to proclaim Jesus Christ crucified and risen. The whole of the New Testament reflects the struggles of the Church in an uncomprehending world. As in those times, people today are searching, searching for what is worthwhile and has real value, for what can really be trusted, for what is really true. People are perplexed and troubled by a world which seems full of anxiety and pain.

St Jerome, who gave us the Latin Vulgate translation of the Scriptures, said: 'If there is anything in this life that sustains a wise person and helps to maintain serenity amid the tribulations and adversities of the world, it is first and foremost I believe the meditation on and knowledge of the Scriptures.' Jerome also said: 'Ignorance of the Scriptures is ignorance of Christ.' The greatest gift we can offer to the people of our time is the good news of Christ, which brings the world new vision and new hope.

This year is the 40th anniversary of *Dei Verbum*, the document of the Second Vatican Council that explained the place of the Scriptures in God's revelation. Since its promulgation Catholics have learnt more than ever before to cherish the Bible. We have rediscovered the Bible as a precious treasure, both ancient and ever new. We have received so much from those who have dedicated their lives to making the Scriptures more accessible to us. The Catholic Church is proud to share the endeavour of bringing Scripture alive with other Christians. The anniversary year of *Dei Verbum* is a good time to turn to the Bible again and to deepen our understanding and love for the Scriptures.

This new millennium, like all beginnings, can be a challenge and an occasion of new hope. Christ has promised to remain with his Church until the end of time. At this time we need to reclaim the Scriptures. The mystery of Christ, of God become man, is the very heart of the Scriptures. As your bishops it is our special duty to help you all to 'grow in the grace and knowledge of our Lord and Saviour Jesus Christ' (*2 Peter* 3:18).

We invite you to read and study this teaching document called *The Gift of Scripture*. It will help you to hear, understand and live God's word. To read the Scriptures regularly and prayerfully is to live continually in the presence of Christ. To come to Christ, to walk with him, is to be his witnesses too in a world that, unknowingly, is searching for the hope that only he can give.

✠ Cormac Cardinal Murphy-O'Connor, Archbishop of Westminster

✠ Keith Cardinal O'Brien, Archbishop of St Andrews and Edinburgh

Introduction

1. A book for today

'Let us take up this book! Let us receive it from the Lord who continually offers it to us through the Church! Let us devour it, so that it can become our very life! Let us savour it deeply: it will make demands of us, but it will give us joy because it is sweet as honey. Filled with hope, we will be able to share it with every man and woman whom we encounter on our way.' (*Ecclesia in Europa* 65) These stirring words are taken from the message of Pope John Paul II to the Church in Europe, in which he challenges our local churches to proclaim a message of hope to the people of today. Many people are fearful and lacking in hope, and this may appear to be justified. There are divisions and conflicts, tensions between religious and ethnic groups, violence between people and wars among the nations. We are faced with various threats to human life, as scientific progress frequently loses sight of the value of the human person. Family ties are weakened, and there is an undermining of solidarity both with those in greatest need and in international affairs as a whole. In spite of such difficulties we Christians remain full of hope, because the word of God in the Scriptures not only assures us of the constant love of God revealed in Jesus Christ, but also shows us the way forward in our troubles. As in past ages and times of turmoil, God still speaks to us in the Holy Scriptures, offering the nourishment and strength we need for the mission we have received. The Bible, which has had such an enormous impact on the life of so many people and nations, has enriched the English language with its momentous words and phrases, and continues to inspire literature, art, music and film. These Holy Scriptures, which have their place at the heart of our liturgy and prayer, remain an extraordinary gift of God for us today.

a message of hope to the people of today

2. The Scriptures in these lands

The people of these islands have a long tradition of love for the Bible. Christianity came to Britain in Roman times, though we do not know who those early bearers of the gospel were. The earliest Christian documents which have survived in these lands are the writings of St Patrick, dating from the fifth century. They show a deep familiarity with the Scriptures. In the fifth century also St Ninian preached the Gospel far and wide from his base in Scotland. In later times saints like Columba, Mungo, Gildas and Cedd travelled far in these islands to spread the Christian faith. The surviving writings of St Gildas show his familiarity with the Scriptures. The great missionary Columbanus and, some time later, St Willibrord and St Boniface brought the light of the gospel to the peoples of continental Europe. Other men and women followed their example. Bede, the tireless historian, monk of Jarrow in the early eighth century and doctor of the Church, as well as completing his great work on the history of the English Church, wrote extensively on the Scriptures, which he called 'the bread of the word'. Sacred Scripture was the foundation of the preaching and writing of Christians in the early centuries.

3. An ancient tradition

We gain a vivid awareness of this love for the Scriptures from the beautiful illuminated manuscripts which still survive, such as the Lindisfarne Gospels, now housed in the British Library, and the Book of Kells, the crowning achievement of Celtic art. In medieval times Sacred Scripture continued to nourish the faith and prayer of the Christian people. Love of Scripture is evident in the writings of the fourteenth-century mystic, Julian of Norwich, and of other medieval mystics. Scripture inspired the ornamentation of medieval churches, with their stained glass windows, wall paintings and statues of biblical figures. Before literacy was common, Christians learned to treasure the Bible from these visual aids, and mystery plays, common in England in the Middle Ages, brought the Bible to life. Both before and after the Reformation, Christians of different communities strove, particularly with the coming of printing, to open up the treasury of the Scriptures for all, sometimes in the face of official disapproval. The Catholic Church of today gratefully acknowledges the contribution of scholars from all Christian communities to the translation, study and exposition of the word of God in the Scriptures.

4. Word and Sacrament

The bishops of England and Wales, and of Scotland, together with the bishops of Ireland, issued a teaching document on the Eucharist, *One Bread, One Body*, in 1998. This new teaching document concerns the Bible, the Holy Scriptures. We know well that Christ comes 'in word and sacrament to strengthen us in holiness' (*Roman Missal*). We are fed by the sacrament, but also by the word. We are invited to 'take and eat', to 'take and drink', but also to 'take and read'. One of the great documents of the Second Vatican Council, which met between 1962 and 1965, is the *Dogmatic Constitution on Divine Revelation*. It is better known by the first two words with which the original Latin text begins, *Dei Verbum*, 'the word of God'. *Dei Verbum* teaches that we continually receive 'the bread of life from the table both of the word of God and of the Body of Christ' (*Dei Verbum* 21). In this third Christian millennium we, the bishops of England and Wales, and of Scotland, offer this new teaching document on the Bible firstly to Catholics, but also to all those who are drawn to the Holy Scriptures, so that they may engage with the Scriptures more deeply and more fruitfully.

5. Scripture and the Church

In the Acts of the Apostles we read the story of how Philip met an Ethiopian who was travelling from Jerusalem to Gaza, reading from the Book of Isaiah. Philip asked him: 'Do you understand what you are reading?' The Ethiopian's answer was: 'How can I unless someone guides me?' (*Acts* 8:30-31) We are well aware that the Scriptures are not always easy to understand. We approach the Scriptures with reverence asking for the enlightenment of that same Spirit who inspired their writing. We approach the Scriptures as members of the family of the Church, seeking the guidance of the living Tradition of the teaching Church. We are more and more aware that Scripture and Tradition are closely bound together, coming from 'the same divine source' (*Dei Verbum* 9). With this document we wish to assist people to welcome the Scriptures as a most precious gift of God to the Church.

6. The layout of the document

This teaching document will make extensive use of the Council document, *Dei Verbum*, published in 1965. In Part One of our document, 'Hearing the word of God', we provide a panorama of God's reaching out to us in the history of salvation. God speaks to us in creation and in revelation. God, who spoke to the people of Israel throughout their history, speaks in the fulness of time through Jesus, the Son. In Part Two, 'Understanding the word of God', we consider the most important characteristics of this word of God as found in the Scriptures. What is this word like? How should we interpret it? What does it mean to describe it as 'God's word in human language'? In Parts Three and Four, 'Reading the Old Testament' and 'Reading the New Testament', we provide a survey of the whole Bible to consider the immense variety of the writings found there, to suggest how they are relevant to our lives today, and to say something about the difficulties encountered in the interpretation of certain texts. In Part Five, 'Living the word of God', we consider the use of the Bible in the Church today, in our liturgy and preaching, in our prayer and catechesis. We suggest practical ways of enhancing our engagement with the Holy Scriptures.

7. At your word, Lord!

In his Apostolic Letter for the beginning of the new millennium, *Novo Millennio Ineunte*, Pope John Paul II offered us a meditation on the passage in the Gospel of Luke where Jesus calls his first disciples. Peter and his companions have laboured all night at their nets and caught nothing, but Jesus tells them to put out into the deep. Peter's reply is: 'At your word I will let down the nets.' (*Luke* 5:5) Peter is willing to respond to Christ and set off in a new direction. Christ challenges us today to be his disciples, for 'Christ, the Son of God made man, is the Father's one, perfect and unsurpassable Word.' (*Catechism of the Catholic Church* 65)

Part One
Hearing the word of God

He sends out his word to the earth.
(*Psalm* 147:15)

8. God's loving initiative

'Long ago God spoke to our ancestors in many and varied ways by the prophets.' (*Hebrews* 1:1) Our Christian faith affirms that God communicates with us. This communication, which we know as 'divine revelation', begins long before the coming of Christ. As the Letter to the Hebrews asserts, men and women came gradually and in various ways to know God through hearing the voice of God. They came to know God as one who desired communion of life with them. It was due to love that God reached out to us. *Dei Verbum* solemnly declares that 'the invisible God, out of the abundance of his love, addresses people as friends and converses with them, to invite them to communion with him and to receive them into that communion' (*Dei Verbum* 2). This revelation of God takes place in the actions and words of God in history. The God who in the beginning created all things by the word continued through the centuries to care for the chosen people, so that they came to know the one true God and to await a Saviour.

9. The Son, the fulness of all revelation

'In these last days God has spoken to us by the Son.' (*Hebrews* 1:2) In the Son of God this revelation reaches its climax, for he is 'both the mediator and the fulness of all revelation' (*Dei Verbum* 2). The Catechism explains: 'Through all the words of Sacred Scripture, God speaks only one single Word, his one Utterance in whom he expresses himself completely.' (*Catechism of the Catholic Church* 102) Jesus Christ confirms what revelation proclaims, namely 'that God is with us to free us from the darkness of sin and death, and to raise us up to eternal life' (*Dei Verbum* 4). By his death and resurrection from the dead, Christ, the Word of God, brings us the good news of God's love. Whoever comes to knowledge of Christ, comes to knowledge of the Father by the gift of the Holy Spirit. In this way we come to know God as Father, Son and Holy Spirit. God is revealed to us through Christ and God's will for our salvation is made known to us. Our response to God's Word is a response of faith, which leads on to thanksgiving and praise (*Dei Verbum* 5).

10. Scripture and Tradition

God's revelation, which came to its fulness in Christ, the Word of God, was handed on from generation to generation and reached written form in the books of the Bible. The prophet Isaiah instructed his disciples to preserve his teaching by writing it down for future generations (*Isaiah* 8:16). St Paul speaks of receiving and handing on in his preaching the fundamental beliefs about Christ (*1 Corinthians* 15:1-3). In such ways we see the emergence of the Tradition, which comes to signify all that has been revealed and handed on concerning Christian faith and life. The Second Vatican Council speaks of Tradition as follows: 'Now what was handed on by the apostles includes all those things which contribute towards the holiness of life and the increase of faith of the people of God, so that the Church, in her teaching, life and worship, perpetuates and hands on to all generations everything that she is, everything that she believes.' (*Dei Verbum* 8) In recent years Christians of different communities in dialogue have explored together the close relationship between Scripture and Tradition. An Agreed Statement by the Second Anglican - Roman Catholic International Commission declares: 'Within Tradition the Scriptures occupy a unique and normative place and belong to what has been given once for all.' (*The Gift of Authority* 19). A Report of the Joint Commission for Dialogue between the Roman

a continuous learning and receiving of new insights

Catholic Church and the World Methodist Council reads: 'The Word is present in Tradition as the communication of the Gospel to new generations of believers.' And again: 'Since they preserve the proclamation of the news of salvation by the prophets and apostles, the Scriptures are at the same time the model and the heart of the Tradition.' (*Speaking the Truth in Love* 18) Scripture and Tradition, closely bound together, make 'present and fruitful in the Church the mystery of Christ' (*Catechism of the Catholic Church* 80).

11. A living Tradition

The Second Vatican Council explains that the Tradition is not something stagnant, but alive and growing, and that it develops in various ways, through contemplation and study, through deepening understanding of spiritual matters, and through the authoritative preaching of the bishops (*Dei Verbum* 8). The Fathers of the Church, the teachers of the faith in the early centuries, testify to the vigour of the Tradition. An early development within the Tradition was the discernment of the canon of Scripture, the complete list of biblical books (*The Gift of Authority* 22). In the continuing Tradition, based on the Scriptures, God still speaks to the Church today and the Holy Spirit of God leads us onwards on the way of truth (*John* 16:13, *Dei Verbum* 8). In recent years, for example, we have seen considerable developments of Catholic teaching on various social issues, such as respect for human life from conception to death, and the need for solidarity with the poor in a globalised world. In dealing with new situations it is essential to listen to God's word with an attentive mind and heart. There is a continuous learning and receiving of new insights through attentiveness to the Scriptures and to the Tradition of the Church. Scripture and the living Tradition are intimately related, coming 'from the same divine source', and they have the same goal (*Dei Verbum* 9). They must each be 'accepted and honoured with equal devotion and reverence' (*Dei Verbum* 9), for they constitute the 'one sacred deposit of the word of God entrusted to the Church' (*Dei Verbum* 10). All disciples of Christ are called to carry forward this precious gift of God for future generations.

12. The role of the Magisterium

In the Acts of the Apostles we read that the early Christians 'devoted themselves to the apostles' teaching and fellowship, to the breaking of bread and the prayers' (*Acts* 2:42). We continue today to live as God's people, as the Church of Christ, in fidelity to the word of God. The task of safeguarding the understanding of the word of God is given to the teaching authority of the Church, the bishops in union with the Pope. Their duty is to serve the word, by teaching it, listening to it attentively, protecting it conscientiously and explaining it faithfully (*Dei Verbum* 10). The teaching authority, or Magisterium, seeks to ensure that new insights are faithful to the word of God. The Second Vatican Council explains: 'It is clear, therefore, that Sacred Tradition, Sacred Scripture and the teaching authority of the Church, in accord with God's most wise design, are so linked and joined together that one cannot stand without the others, and that they all together, each in its own way under the action of the one Holy Spirit, contribute effectively to the salvation of souls.' (*Dei Verbum* 10)

Part Two
Understanding the word of God

Was there ever a word so great?
(*Deuteronomy* 4:32)

13. God's word in human language

God communicates with us out of love, and in so doing adapts the word to our human situation. A basic insight in understanding the gift of Scripture is that God's word is expressed in human language (*Dei Verbum* 11). This realisation presents a challenge. How are we to give proper acknowledgement both to the divine reality of the word of God in Scripture and to its human dimensions? Not to recognise the divine reality of Scripture would be to fail to venerate it as the inspired word of God. Not to recognise the human features of Scripture would lead us into fundamentalism, which brings a reluctance to ask deeper questions about the text. Such an approach has little interest in the historical origins and development of Scripture and thereby impedes understanding of the gradual revelation of the word of God in changing historical situations. The realisation that God's word comes in human form goes back to earliest times, but modern study of the Bible has made great progress in working out the implications of this insight.

14. The truth of Scripture

The Scriptures themselves proclaim that they are inspired by God, that God is their author, and that they were written by the inspiration of the Holy Spirit. Just as the prophets were inspired by the Spirit of God to proclaim the word, so too 'all Scripture is inspired by God and is useful for teaching, for reproof, for correction, and for training in

The Gift of Scripture

righteousness' (*2 Timothy* 3:16). On the basis of usage and acceptance in the Church, it was gradually determined which books were to be regarded as inspired. These books were to be listed as Holy Scripture and became 'canonical', fundamental to the rule of faith. The decision about which books to include in the canon of Scripture reflected the faith of the whole people. The books thus declared canonical and inspired by the Spirit of God contain 'the truth which God wished to be set down in the sacred writings for the sake of our salvation' (*Dei Verbum* 11). It is important to note this teaching of the Second Vatican Council that the truth of Scripture is to be found in all that is written down 'for the sake of our salvation'. We should not expect total accuracy from the Bible in other, secular matters. We should not expect to find in Scripture full scientific accuracy or complete historical precision.

15. The inspiration of Scripture

God is the author of Scripture, but the sacred authors are also true authors. How does this come about? The text of *Dei Verbum* affirms that God 'acted in and through' the sacred writers (*Dei Verbum* 11). Inspiration should be seen as an extraordinary action of the Holy Spirit in the mind and heart of those involved in the production of the Scriptures. With our awareness that the biblical material often went through long periods of oral tradition before reaching written form, we must affirm that the inspiration of the Holy Spirit was at work in these stages too, guiding the minds and hearts of all those who were involved in the development of the material. We should also acknowledge the inspiration of God's Spirit working in the communities, both Jewish and Christian, from whom the scriptural material emerged. Nevertheless, the full richness of the charism of inspiration operates in the mind and heart of the writer of the final text. Ultimately, the inspiration of Scripture remains a mystery of God's loving outreach to us, a mystery which we cannot fully fathom.

16. A parallel with the Incarnation

From the early centuries of the Christian faith, the Fathers of the Church and theologians have acknowledged that God's word comes to us in human form. St John Chrysostom, that great Father of the

Eastern Church, refers frequently to the 'divine condescension' by which the words of God are adapted to our limited human understanding. *Dei Verbum* follows Chrysostom in drawing a parallel between the Incarnation of the Son of God and the human expression of the words of God: 'For the words of God, expressed in human language, have been made like human discourse, just as once the Word of the eternal Father, when he took to himself the flesh of human weakness, was made like human beings.' (*Dei Verbum* 13). Our God comes willingly to be immersed in our humanity. The Son comes to live human life to the full, and the words of God share fully in the dynamics of human language.

17. The human dimensions of Scripture

It follows that in order to understand the word of God in Scripture we should seek to know the intention of the human author. In this endeavour we can learn from those who developed techniques for understanding other ancient literature. These techniques generally come under the title of 'the historical-critical method'. The document of the Pontifical Biblical Commission, *The Interpretation of the Bible in the Church*, published in 1993, surveys the various techniques used in this method and evaluates them, as well as providing a detailed review of other methods and approaches to the Bible. The most crucial question is this: what kind of writing did the human writer employ in order to communicate God's word? Here we come to the important question of the 'literary genres' employed in the Scriptures. The appreciation of the literary genre being used is a major tool for correct understanding of the text. In his ground-breaking encyclical on the Bible, *Divino Afflante Spiritu*, published in 1943, Pope Pius XII encouraged interpreters of Scripture to explore the literary genres in use among the ancient people of the East in order to determine what similar kinds of writing were employed by the writers of the Scriptures. *Dei Verbum* confirms that such questions should be asked of the whole of Scripture (*Dei Verbum* 12). We need to be aware both of the kinds of writing in use among those who wrote the Scriptures, and of the genres employed by other ancient

> *our God comes willingly to be immersed in our humanity*

peoples (*Dei Verbum* 12). This research has borne fruit over many years. Significant efforts have been made, for example, to determine the precise nature of the writings we call 'gospels'.

18. The unity of Scripture

Exploration of the human dimensions of the Scriptures allows us to discover the divine message. In so doing we need to invoke the assistance of the Holy Spirit, who inspired these writings. In this way we acknowledge the Scriptures for what they really are, the word of God in human language, inspired by the Spirit of God. We should also not isolate particular texts and understandings from the rest of Scripture, but should be attentive to the content and unity of the whole of Scripture (*Dei Verbum* 12). Understanding texts in the context of the whole Bible means that we are able to hear the word of God in its fulness. In particular, we read the Jewish Scriptures with new insight due to the fulfilment brought by Christ, which is displayed in the books of the New Testament.

19. The danger of fundamentalism

The phenomenon of fundamentalism is prevalent in today's world, bringing with it an intransigent intolerance which rules out both listening to other views and the willingness to dialogue. There are significant dangers involved in a fundamentalist approach to the Scriptures. Fundamentalist reading will often focus on a particular text or texts, and disregard others which express different perspectives, thus making absolute what is a partial and incomplete understanding within Scripture. Such an approach is dangerous, for example, when people of one nation or group see in the Bible a mandate for their own superiority, and even consider themselves permitted by the Bible to use violence against others. The fundamentalist approach disregards the diversity of views and the development of understanding which is found in the Bible and does not allow for the presence of 'imperfect and time-conditioned elements' within Scripture (*Dei Verbum* 15). 'Fundamentalism actually invites people to a kind of intellectual suicide' (*Interpretation of the Bible* I.F), for it favours a superficial interpretation of biblical texts, in which there is insufficient consideration of the place of a given text within a developing tradition. Fundamentalism will often take a simplistic view of literary genre, as when narrative texts which are of a more complex nature are treated as historical (*Interpretation of the Bible* I.F). In essence, fundamentalist reading disregards the various human dimensions of the Scriptures, and thereby undervalues the gift of Scripture and the 'divine condescension' which gives us God's word in human language.

20. The dynamism of Scripture

Centuries of reflection and prayer have led Christians to discover new truths and new senses of biblical passages. Catholic teaching has treasured the 'spiritual sense' of Scripture, which has been defined as 'the meaning expressed by the biblical texts when read, under the influence of the Holy Spirit, in the context of the paschal mystery of Christ and of the new life which flows from it' (*Interpretation of the Bible* II.B.2). Later understandings go beyond the intention of the original human authors. Material concerning the promised Messiah, for example, was understood in a new and fuller way when Christ came. Catholic teaching has spoken of a 'fuller sense', the *sensus plenior*. Such fuller understandings have their basis in the fact that the text itself is often richer than the author's intention and contains potentialities which the Holy Spirit actuates in the course of history. Modern insights about the nature of language have explored and clarified the potential of the written word to give rise to new meanings and insights through reading in new contexts and times (*Interpretation of the Bible* II.A). The 'fuller sense' can be attributed to a biblical text by 'a subsequent biblical author' or by 'an authentic doctrinal tradition or a conciliar definition' (*Interpretation of the Bible* II.B.3). Biblical commentators also use the term 're-reading' when they refer to later understandings within the Bible itself of earlier texts (*Interpretation of the Bible* III.A.1).

21. The Fathers of the Church

Catholics have always valued the senses of Scripture explained by the Fathers of the Church and spiritual writers through the centuries. Such commentaries on Scripture illustrate the richness of the Bible and continue to nourish the Church. The understanding of the unity of all Scripture among the Fathers of the Church led them to pay less attention to the historical development of revelation, and they often see, for example, hidden christological meanings even in the details of Scripture.

Their use of such 'allegorical' interpretation can often seem exaggerated, but the Fathers nevertheless teach us to read the Bible with an authentic Christian spirit (*Interpretation of the Bible* III.B.2). In our own times there is a renewed interest in the study of these ancient commentaries. This is to be welcomed and encouraged, for it demonstrates an increasing appreciation of the developing tradition of the Church both among Catholics and other Christians.

22. The rule of faith

As the Tradition developed, the Fathers, such as St Irenaeus, began to speak of the 'rule of faith' (*regula fidei*). They provided summaries of the principal teachings of the faith, based on the Scriptures. This developing understanding of Scripture in no way implies a disregard for the literal meaning of the texts, which is reached by searching for the intention of the human author, nor does it downplay the importance of the historical-critical method. We must at the same time have full regard for the 'analogy of faith', which means that we understand each passage of Scripture in the harmony and coherence of all the truths of faith (*Dei Verbum* 12, *Catechism of the Catholic Church* 114).

23. A balanced approach

To understand the Scriptures better we must then fully acknowledge that they are 'the word of God in human language'. God is their author, and the sacred writers are also true authors. Both dimensions must be honoured, as Pope John Paul II has taught: 'Catholic exegesis does not focus its attention only on the human aspects of biblical revelation, which is sometimes the mistake of the historical-critical method, nor only on the divine aspects, as fundamentalism would have it; it strives to highlight both of them, united as they are in the divine 'condescension' (*Dei Verbum* 13), which is at the foundation of all Scripture.' (*De tout Coeur* 14). We treasure and marvel at God's reaching out to us through what is human: in the Incarnation of the Son of God, the Word made flesh, and in the human expression of God's word.

God reaches out to us through what is human

Part Three
Reading the Old Testament

Your words became to me a joy and the delight of my heart. (Jeremiah 15:16)

24. An immense collection

We begin our journey through the Bible with the Scriptures of Judaism, which Christians know as the Old Testament. An immense collection of forty-six books was gathered together over many centuries. Each book has its own history of composition, and much of the material will have existed in oral form before ever being written down, at which point it was ordered and edited in various ways. Modern study has made us more aware of the complexity of the processes of composition involved. We believe that all these processes were safeguarded by the inspiration of the Holy Spirit.

25. The canon

The document of the Pontifical Biblical Commission, *The Jewish People and their Sacred Scriptures in the Christian Bible*, published in 2001, describes the emergence of the canon, the official list of inspired books, which developed over a long period (*The Jewish People* 16-18). By the time of Jesus those parts of the canon which are known as the Torah and the Prophets were already completed, and Jesus repeatedly refers to them (*Matthew* 5:17, 7:12; *Luke* 24:44). The Torah is the Hebrew name for what Christian tradition has referred to as the Law. The Hebrew word *torah* is more accurately translated as 'teaching' or 'instruction' and is the name given to the five books we call the *Pentateuch*. In Jewish tradition the Prophets (or *nebi'im* in Hebrew) include the historical books of

Joshua, Judges, 1 and 2 Samuel, and 1 and 2 Kings, in addition to the major and minor prophets. A third category of books, known simply as 'writings' (Hebrew *ketubim*), was still an open collection at the time of Jesus. The Jewish religious leadership would not finally close its canon until the second or third century AD (*The Jewish People* 16).

26. The deuterocanonical books

Meanwhile, after the conquests of Alexander the Great, who died in 323 BC, the Greek language had spread throughout the eastern Mediterranean and Jews in Egypt had translated their Hebrew Scriptures into Greek and produced the Greek bible known as the Septuagint. It contained books which never found their way into the Hebrew canon, the so-called deuterocanonical books: Tobit, Judith, 1 and 2 Maccabees, Wisdom, Ecclesiasticus (*Sirach*) and Baruch. The writers of the New Testament freely used these books and the Church came to adopt a canon of Jewish books longer than the Hebrew canon (*The Jewish People* 17). Indeed, from late patristic times onwards, both the Greek and the Latin Church included the deuterocanonical books in their liturgical readings. From time to time the presence of these extra books was contested in the Church, but wide usage and a developing consensus held them to be of equal status to the books of the Hebrew canon (*The Jewish People* 18). The deuterocanonical books were challenged at the time of the Reformation, and known by some Christians as 'apocrypha', books of a lesser status than Sacred Scripture. In recent times, however, there has been an increasing use of the deuterocanonical books, and they can often be found in editions of the Bible not produced by Catholics.

27. The Old Testament

The title 'Old Testament' originates from the writings of St Paul (*2 Corinthians* 3:14). This title has sometimes been considered somewhat negative and has been replaced by terms such as 'the First Testament' and 'the Jewish Scriptures' in order to avoid any possible offence. No lack of reverence or negative connotation is signified by the title 'Old Testament', for these books are an essential part of the Christian Bible (*The Jewish People* 19 note 33). The words 'Old Testament' simply make clear for Christians the distinction between the books of the Jewish Scriptures and the books of the new covenant brought about by the death and resurrection of Christ, which we refer to as the 'New Testament'.

28. In the beginning
The Scriptures of Judaism begin in the Book of Genesis with chapters which 'set the tone for reading the entire Bible' (*The Jewish People* 27). The opening eleven chapters of Genesis focus on the situation of the world and of human beings, created in the image and likeness of God and yet distant from God through sin. The goodness of the creator God is set alongside the human need for salvation. These opening chapters consider the predicament of the whole human race, not simply of the Jewish people. Since the questions asked and answers given here concern all people, it is not surprising that certain similarities are found between these religious stories of the early chapters of Genesis and traditional material from other cultures, notably from the ancient East. The discovery of such material led the Church to develop her teaching concerning the literary genres found in the Bible. It became clear that the material found in these chapters of Genesis could not simply be described as historical writing. Though they may contain some historical traces, the primary purpose was to provide religious teaching (*The Jewish People* 27-28). These chapters continue to teach us about the goodness and providence of the creator God, the devastating effects of human collusion with evil, the entrusting of the earth to human beings and their duty to care for it, the dignity and equality of men and women made in the image of God, and the divine command to keep the sabbath holy.

29. A chosen people
Once we reach chapter 12 of the Book of Genesis attention is focussed on the ancient ancestors of the Jewish people and on the patriarch Abraham. 'The most loving God, carefully planning and preparing the salvation of the whole human race, by a special commitment chose for himself a people to whom he would entrust his promises.' (*Dei Verbum* 14). *Dei Verbum* explains that the choice of Israel is the first stage of the plan of God for the salvation of all peoples. Abraham is

The Gift of Scripture

the recipient of God's promises and of God's free gifts, the man of faith who trusts that God will provide for him (*Genesis* 15:6, 22:8). The apostle Paul commends him as a model for Christian belief. He is remembered as 'father of many nations' (*Romans* 4:18) and is commemorated in the liturgy as 'our father in faith' (*Roman Missal, First Eucharistic Prayer*). The patriarchs and matriarchs of Genesis are people of faith (*Hebrews* 11:8-22). They hear the word of God and they live by it. From them the revelation of God will become known to the peoples of the earth. Both Old and New Testaments teach acceptance of the peoples of all nations as children of the one God (*The Jewish People* 33-35). This teaching of Scripture is of extraordinary relevance today.

30. The exodus and the covenant

Central to the Jewish Scriptures and fundamental to the faith of Jews to this day is the exodus from slavery in Egypt (*The Jewish People* 31). God is revealed to Israel by 'words and deeds' which are closely connected (*Dei Verbum* 2 and 14). God reveals himself to Moses as 'I am who I am' (*Exodus* 3:14). The providential action of God in delivering his people from slavery and the story of the giving of the law and the making of a covenant at Sinai are the focus of the Book of Exodus. Moses is mediator for the people and the trusted servant of God (*Numbers* 12:7). The covenant between God and the people is summarised in the words: 'I will be your God, and you shall be my people.' (*Leviticus* 26:12). Israel is to live totally and exclusively for God (*The Jewish People* 37-38). The laws of the covenant were developed over many centuries and are revered by the Jewish people as the great gift of Torah.

31. Laws of life

Jews today continue to celebrate the Passover year by year as they relive the liberation from Egypt. That God freed the people from slavery is the central tenet of Jewish faith. The Lord God then gives them a law to direct their lives (*Exodus* 20:1-17). The Torah is the part of the Scriptures most revered by Jews (*The Jewish People* 43). For Christians, the liberation from Egypt is a preparation for the liberation of all people from slavery to sin and death, the liberation won by Jesus Christ. The God who wants the Israelites to live in freedom desires freedom for all people. The Jewish Torah contains much that remains valid for Christians. Christians consider the Ten Commandments, or Decalogue, to have fundamental and enduring validity. The Decalogue is a 'path to life' and has a 'liberating power' (*Catechism of the Catholic Church* 2057). The social legislation of the Pentateuch teaches respect for all, equality of treatment, and a bias in favour of vulnerable people, such as the widow, the orphan and the stranger. Such teaching has

the loving God calls people to live in love, truth and justice

a profound relevance for us today, when the problems of the world's poor fail to be addressed with appropriate urgency. Social concern is carried forward by prophets, such as Amos and Isaiah, by the teaching of Jesus, who reaches out to the poor, the sick and the excluded, and by the social teaching of the Church over the centuries. But Christian faith also announces freedom from the old law, and a new life by the law of the Spirit (*Romans* 8:1-2). For Jesus, who comes to bring the law to fulfilment, the two greatest commandments are love of God and love of neighbour (*Mark* 12:28-34; *Matthew* 5:17). There is a profound agreement between the teaching of Jesus and the New Testament, on the one hand, and the fundamentals of the Torah, on the other hand. For both Jew and Christian the loving God calls people to live in love, truth and justice.

32. The promised land

The story of Israel continues in the books known as 'historical' by Christians and the 'early prophets' by Jews. The books of Joshua and Judges speak in different ways of the settling of Israelites in the land of Canaan, the land which would become the land of Israel. The entry into the promised land is seen as a fulfilment of the divine promise, but the narratives raise serious theological questions. God is presented as commanding the Israelites to annihilate their enemies by inflicting the 'ban' or 'curse of destruction' (*Joshua* 6:17-21). Such commands arise from a theology in which anyone who is not a believer is considered to bring religious contamination to believers (*The Jewish People* 56). When *Dei Verbum* speaks of 'imperfect and time-conditioned elements' in Scripture (*Dei Verbum* 15), it no doubt intends to include the texts concerning the ban. Israel will gradually understand that no people is to be treated in this way and that all peoples are called to know the one God. A further difficult text is the story of the sacrifice of his daughter by the judge Jephthah in chapter 11 of the Book of Judges. It is essential to see such texts in their historical context, so that primitive ideas about God's demands are balanced by the truths and the values which emerge from the later Scriptures. As far as the promised land is concerned, Christians see its fulfilment in the promise of the Kingdom (*Hebrews* 3:7-4:11, *The Jewish People* 57, *Interpretation of the Bible* III.A.1).

33. The kingship

Once the Israelites are settled in the promised land the question of kingship arises. The First Book of Samuel tells of the controversy among the people of Israel concerning the institution of a monarchy. Should the people of God be ruled by a king? Does God's sovereignty forbid this? Israel comes to understand the kingship of David and his descendants to be given by God as a guarantee of God's continuing solidarity with the people (*2 Samuel* 7:15-16). A related issue is that of the building of the temple. After initial doubts about constructing for God a temple like those of pagan gods, David's son Solomon builds and solemnly dedicates the temple in Jerusalem as the place of which God said 'My name shall be there.' (*1 Kings* 8:29) There is a keen awareness that no building built by human hands could ever house the living God (*1 Kings* 8:27). The presentation of kingship in the books of 1 and 2 Kings is a history of the infidelity of the majority of kings with a few notable exceptions. A parallel history in the books of Chronicles enhances the presentation of David and of his son Solomon.

34. The prophets of Israel

Throughout the period of the monarchy and in later centuries prophets speak the word of God to Israel. Some prophets, such as Samuel, Nathan and Elijah, appear in the historical books of 1 and 2 Samuel and 1 and 2 Kings, while the major and minor prophets have books attributed to them. These books are known as the 'later prophets' in Jewish tradition. It is the task of the prophet to speak for God to individuals and more usually to the people. The prophets do not so much foretell the future as speak with devastating clarity about the realities they see around them. A prophet may well have to reprimand the people for their sins (*The Jewish People* 52). Prophets such as Amos and Isaiah recall the covenant obligations of Israel, challenging the people to live by them and fiercely proclaiming their concern for the poor and the weak. Disasters are threatened for those who continue to oppress their fellows, and also for rulers who fail to trust in God. The prophets will also give encouragement and hope to the people, particularly at the time of the exile in Babylon, when Jerusalem and the temple have been destroyed and everything seems hopeless. It falls to the exilic prophets to proclaim hope and new life to people who await only death (*The Jewish People* 58). For Christians these prophecies of salvation herald the full salvation eventually brought to all by Christ, and still speak powerfully of new life and redemption.

35. The suffering of the prophets

Prophets are called by God and inspired by the Spirit of God. The books of Isaiah, Jeremiah and Ezekiel provide narratives of their calling (*Isaiah* 6; *Jeremiah* 1; *Ezekiel* 1-3). Amid intense experiences of God and of their own unworthiness, they are given strength for their mission. Prophets are often unwelcome and fall victim to violence. Jeremiah is put in the stocks, thrown into a cistern, and kept prisoner due to his preaching of submission to Babylon at the time of the siege of Jerusalem (*Jeremiah* 20 and 37-38). A scroll of his words is destroyed by the king (*Jeremiah* 36). Despite such vulnerability the power of prophecy lives on. Jesus is presented in the gospels as a prophet who is at times acclaimed, but whose message is unwelcome to many (*Matthew* 21:11; *Mark* 6:4). Countless men and women have continued to proclaim the word throughout the centuries, for God still gives the courage once given to the prophets to those who proclaim true values to an often unheeding world.

36. Prophecy and fulfilment

Christian treatment of the books of the prophets has particularly highlighted prophetic words about the future king, the Messiah or 'anointed one'. The hopes of Israel for such a God-given ruler are expressed particularly by the prophet Isaiah (*Isaiah* 9 and 11). The poems of the 'suffering servant' in the later part of the Book of Isaiah (*Isaiah* 42, 49, 50 and 52-53) have been treasured by Christians as foreseeing the suffering and death of Christ. The Christian emphasis on such texts has led sometimes to a reduced appreciation of the other dimensions of the prophetic preaching, such as the social teaching. Significant though it is, the messianic hope is not a dominant feature in the books of the prophets, but in the New Testament it becomes 'an essential and basic interpretative key' (*The Jewish People* 63). The New Testament writers demonstrate the fulfilment brought by Christ by adopting and developing elements from the Hebrew Scriptures. There is continuity in fulfilment, but at the same time a new and fuller sense is discovered in the ancient words (*The Jewish People* 21).

37. The Wisdom literature

The Hebrew Scriptures also contain books known generically as 'writings' (Hebrew *ketubim*). For Christians many of these remaining books are categorised as 'wisdom literature'. The term is a loose designation but certainly would include Job, Proverbs, Ecclesiastes (*Qoheleth*) and the deuterocanonical books of Ecclesiasticus (*Sirach*) and the Wisdom of Solomon (*Book of Wisdom*). These books share an appreciation of the divine gift of 'wisdom', sometimes personified as a woman inviting people to a rich banquet (*Proverbs* 9:1-6). This fine collection of books considers in a variety of ways a multitude of issues faced by human beings. Wise traditional sayings are gathered together in the Book of Proverbs, some of which may well date back to the time of king Solomon, reputed to be the wisest of kings. Some proverbs are profound and weighty, while others are somewhat trivial. The multiform insights of the human mind are acknowledged as owing something to the inspiration of God. The Song of Songs should also be mentioned here. This collection of poems about human love has nourished our understanding of the love of God for the people, and the love of Christ for the Church.

38. The problem of suffering

The Book of Job is a fine and precious book, a masterpiece of Hebrew poetry and a major landmark in religious thought. It tackles the most troubling question for believers, the plight of the innocent who suffer. While earlier books had simply explained all suffering, whether personal or collective, as brought about by sin, Job stands firm in refuting such easy answers. His friends relentlessly repeat the traditional theology, but Job persists in proclaiming his innocence and is rewarded with two speeches from God (*Job* 38-42). The speeches seem to teach that human beings cannot fathom the plan of God, that God bestows freedom on all creatures, and that evil is somehow bound up with this freedom. In response, Job humbly admits that he cannot understand the depths of God's ways (*Job* 42:1-3). The Book of Job is a fine example of how the Scriptures may reflect a process of learning and a development of understanding among people. The book encourages deeper reflection on the mystery of suffering, which is most profoundly presented for Christians in the agony and cross of Jesus.

39. The Psalms

The Jewish Scriptures contain 'wonderful treasuries of prayer' (*Dei Verbum* 15), and among these the Book of Psalms is the finest. The Psalms have been described as the 'very heart of the Old Testament' (*The Jewish People* 47). Prayed by Jews and Christians over thousands of years, these wonderful hymns emerge from so many human emotions and situations. They can be used in time of sorrow to express personal pain, or associate with the pain of others. Such laments will often end with a glimpse of the healing power of God and lead to thanksgiving, as can be seen so well in Psalm 22 (21). Some psalms even contain the language of hatred and violence, and, while these 'cursing psalms' are not often used in our liturgy, their presence in our Bible teaches us that even strong emotions can be expressed to the God who knows our hearts. Deep emotions can be admitted before God, for it is the acting out of such hatred which cannot be condoned. The Christian who recites these verses today may apply such prayers not to personal enemies but to all those forces which seek to undermine the coming of God's Kingdom. Hymns of trust such as Psalm 23 (22) retain enormous popularity. This psalm presents God to us as a caring shepherd and a generous host who provides a banquet, and speaks of the steadfast love and constancy of the God we come to know more fully in the Son, who is called the 'Good Shepherd'. The Book of Psalms contains jubilant hymns of praise of God. The final psalms are punctuated by the repeated cry of 'Hallelujah! Praise the Lord!' (*Psalms* 146-150).

40. Apocalyptic visions

Standing on the threshold of the New Testament, the Book of Daniel, though placed among the prophets by Christian usage, is a unique book, which contains enigmatic visions. It was written for a persecuted people to assure them of God's unending care, and reassures the oppressed and persecuted in any age that evil cannot finally triumph. This is a new kind of writing, known as 'apocalyptic', which will also be found in the New Testament Book of Revelation (*The Jewish People* 60). The book speaks of the coming of the kingdom of God (*Daniel* 2:44), and proclaims the reward of resurrection for those who are faithful (*Daniel* 12:1-3). It prepares for the coming of Christ.

41. God's patient teaching

This survey of the books of the Old Testament shows how God's revelation gradually brings people to a deeper and richer understanding (*Dei Verbum* 14). 'The divine pedagogy has taken a group of people where it found them and led them patiently in the direction of an ideal union with God and towards a moral integrity which our modern society is still far from attaining.' (*The Jewish People* 87) The journey is slow and difficult because that is the nature of human learning and human growth (*The Jewish People* 21). Each of us is called to tread this ancient path,

the journey brings us to the New Testament and to Christ

encouraged by the examples of faith of so many individuals and communities. The journey leads us through the Old Testament, the Scriptures of the Jewish faith which became part of the Christian Bible, and brings us to the New Testament and to Christ. The Church has always strongly rejected the suggestion that the Old Testament should be discarded or neglected: 'Without the Old Testament, the New Testament would be an incomprehensible book, a plant deprived of its roots and destined to dry up and wither.' (*The Jewish People* 84)

Part Four
Reading the New Testament

The word of the Lord endures for ever. That word is the good news which was announced to you. (1 Peter 1:25)

42. The climax of revelation
'The word of God, which is the power of God for the salvation of all believers (*Rom* 1:16), is set forth and displays its strength in an outstanding way in the writings of the New Testament.' (*Dei Verbum* 17) In these writings we learn how God, who spoke to our ancestors through the prophets, finally speaks through the Son. He comes to proclaim the kingdom of God, to make God known by his actions and words, and to bring the work of salvation to its climax. This he accomplishes by his death and resurrection, by his return to the Father and by the sending of the Holy Spirit. The gospel is preached and the Church is gathered from all the nations (*Dei Verbum* 17; *Catechism of the Catholic Church* 124).

43. The four gospels
The four gospels, the principal testimonies to the life and teaching of Jesus, are 'the heart of all the Scriptures' (*Catechism of the Catholic Church* 125). Among all the Scriptures, even of the New Testament, the gospels have the place of greatest honour, demonstrated by the Church in a variety of ways. In a desire to assist the reverent and life-changing acceptance of the gospels by the men and women of our time the Church has set forth in the *Dogmatic Constitution on Divine*

Revelation (*Dei Verbum*) and in the *Catechism of the Catholic Church* an account of the stages of formation of the gospels. A fuller account of the process is to be found in the document of the Pontifical Biblical Commission on the historicity of the gospels, entitled *Sancta Mater Ecclesia*. The process began with the life and teaching of Jesus himself. Then, after the return of Jesus to the Father, the apostles preached about Jesus with the fuller understanding they enjoyed from their encounters with the risen Lord and their receiving of the Holy Spirit. Finally, the evangelists wrote their gospels, selecting elements from the oral or written tradition, condensing some elements and explaining others in order to assist the situation of the Christian communities, and always proclaiming the good news in such a way as to make known the truth about Jesus (*Dei Verbum* 18-19; *Catechism of the Catholic Church* 126). The four gospels provide four complementary presentations of Jesus. The mystery of Jesus the Messiah and Son of God is so profound and difficult for human minds to fathom that no one portrait of Jesus will do him justice. The Church provides for us four trustworthy accounts from the testimony of the apostles and the developing understanding of the early Christian communities.

44. A unique literary genre

In his Apostolic Letter for the new millennium, Pope John Paul II has given a concise description of the nature of the gospels: 'What we receive from them is a vision of faith based on precise historical testimony: a true testimony which the Gospels, despite their complex redaction and primarily catechetical purpose, pass on to us in an entirely trustworthy way.' (*Novo Millennio Ineunte* 17). In the case of the gospels it is most necessary to respect the nature of the writing and the unique literary genre employed by the evangelists. Differences between the four canonical gospels have been acknowledged from the early centuries and have sometimes been used to challenge the Christian faith. We need to be aware that the gospels are a wonderful weaving together of history and theology, as they report the events of Christ's life intertwined with later understandings of Christ from the communities of the first century. The three synoptic gospels according to Matthew, Mark and Luke

The Gift of Scripture

display such similarities that it is incontrovertible that the evangelists have shared material. Despite the long-held view that the Gospel of Matthew was the first to be written, it is now believed by the vast majority of scholars that Mark's gospel was written first. The Catholic Church has no difficulty with this contention, which seems to have been amply demonstrated by scholars for more than a century. According to this scholarly view, the Gospel of Mark was employed by Matthew and Luke as one source in the composition of their much longer gospels. The Gospel of John stands apart with its own traditions about Jesus and its distinct process of composition. Later 'apocryphal' gospels, many of which have been studied by scholars in recent times, were not added to the Christian canon, for they frequently give exaggerated accounts, and portrayals of Jesus and his teaching which are difficult to reconcile with those found in the four canonical gospels.

the gospels are a wonderful weaving together of history and theology

45. The good news of the kingdom of God

Mark's gospel is traditionally linked to the preaching of St Peter in Rome, and begins with a proclamation of Christian faith. Jesus is described as 'Christ' and 'Son of God' in the opening verse of the gospel as if to remind us that the gospels are primarily catechetical and given to us as preaching. The following verses of Mark continue to provide a rich christology in their presentation of Jesus. He comes as the one who is greater than John the Baptist. He is the sinless one who undergoes John's baptism of repentance with sinful men and women. He is the Spirit-filled Messiah but also the Servant of the Lord. Filled with the Spirit, Jesus is tested by Satan. The first words Jesus speaks in Mark's gospel proclaim the coming of the kingdom, or reign, of God (*Mark* 1:15). This is the central theme of Jesus' preaching in the synoptic gospels, and many of his parables illustrate features of the kingdom (*The Jewish People* 61). Jesus proclaims God's victory, the certain arrival of the reign of God, and he demonstrates the reality of that victory in his mighty deeds, which we describe as miracles. Mark presents them as victories over the power of evil which brings sickness and pain to men and women. The miracles of Jesus are confirmation of his message. Jesus works as God works by both deeds and words.

46. Mark's story of Jesus

Mark has a dramatic way of gathering together the traditions about Jesus. The opening chapters of the gospel (*Mark* 1-8) describe Jesus' ministry in Galilee, where he enjoys some success and gathers disciples together, though the religious authorities are already concerned about his popularity. Mark then has Jesus make the difficult and dangerous journey to Jerusalem, where after a brief ministry he will be arrested, tortured and executed. While Mark reports just one journey of Jesus to Jerusalem, the Gospel of John shows Jesus in Jerusalem at various points and suggests he made several visits to Jerusalem for the great feasts. There is no serious discrepancy here, for Mark has devised a particular structure to enhance the story of Jesus and has arranged his traditional material accordingly. Mark effectively portrays the steadfast commitment of Jesus to do the will of the Father by making the lonely journey to the cross. Matthew and Luke adopt the basic sequence of Mark's gospel, adding much new material.

47. The suffering Messiah

A dialogue between Jesus and Peter in the middle of the Gospel of Mark is considered something of a turning-point. When Jesus asks his disciples who they say he is, Peter declares Jesus to be the Christ, the Messiah (*Mark* 8:29). Quite unexpectedly, Jesus goes on to speak of his arrest and death in Jerusalem. Peter reacts in horror, and, whenever Jesus speaks of his coming death, the disciples are found wanting, not understanding and being afraid to ask. For them, the work of the Messiah should not include martyrdom, but Jesus challenges Jewish expectations about the Messiah (*The Jewish People* 21 and 63). The journey of Jesus to Jerusalem is also a journey of the disciples who accompany him, struggling to come to terms with his fate.

48. The death and resurrection of Jesus
After a brief ministry in Jerusalem, and the Last Supper with his disciples, Jesus is arrested and crucified due to the hostility of the religious leaders and with the collusion of the Roman authorities (*The Jewish People* 72). The suffering and crucifixion of Jesus are presented with great realism by Mark. At Jesus' death it is the Roman centurion who proclaims his greatness (*Mark* 15:39). Mark reports the discovery of the empty tomb and an appendix to the gospel gives a summary of accounts of the appearances of the risen Jesus (*Mark* 16:1-8 and 16:9-20).

49. Matthew's opening chapters
The evangelist Matthew adapts the story of Mark by introducing a considerable amount of new material. This evangelist addresses a community in which the believers are Jewish Christians. It is his primary purpose to demonstrate that Jesus fulfils the Jewish Scriptures. He begins his gospel with a genealogy illustrating the descent of Jesus from Abraham, father of the Jews, and from king David (*The Jewish People* 70). Matthew, unlike Mark, provides stories of the birth of Jesus. They are punctuated by Old Testament citations which are declared to have been brought to fulfilment. These stories highlight the role of Joseph in accepting and protecting Mary's child and, with the coming of the magi, show Jesus to be saviour of all the nations. They also suggest, at the very beginning of the gospel, that the political and religious leaders are hostile to the Messiah.

50. The Sermon on the Mount
Matthew introduces five major speeches of Jesus, setting down in writing in this way much traditional teaching of Jesus. The five speeches are understood to reflect the five books of Moses, the Jewish Torah, which we know as the Pentateuch. Jesus is the new prophet, greater than Moses. The first and greatest of the speeches is the Sermon on the Mount (*Matthew* 5-7). Christians and many others treasure the Beatitudes, with which the Sermon begins, in which we are taught how God turns what the world considers misfortune into channels of blessing. God looks with love on the poor and the gentle, the merciful and the pure in heart. Jesus declares solemnly that he has

come to bring the law and the prophets to fulfilment and demonstrates this in his authoritative teaching. Jesus develops Jewish teaching on tenets of the law and on almsgiving, fasting and prayer, the traditional good works among the Jews. The Sermon contains the challenge of Jesus to be 'perfect as your heavenly Father is perfect' (*Matthew* 5:48), a challenge with us to this day.

51. Jews and Christians in Matthew
While on the one hand stressing that Jesus brings the Scriptures to fulfilment, Matthew also reflects the distance between Christians and Jews which was part of the experience of his community. The antagonism between the Jewish Christians and Jews who did not accept Jesus has profoundly influenced the gospel. Jesus' opposition to the scribes and Pharisees is dramatically stressed (*Matthew* 23). Such antagonistic words must never be used as a pretext to treat members of the Jewish people with contempt. The words of the crowd 'His blood be on us and on our children!' (*Matthew* 27:25) are an example of dramatic exaggeration, and must never be used, as they have in past centuries with tragic consequences, to encourage hatred and persecution of the Jewish people. The attitudes and language of first century quarrels between Jews and Jewish Christians should never again be emulated in relations between Jews and Christians (*The Jewish People* 70-71).

> Jesus brings the law and the prophets to fulfilment

52. Matthew and the Church
Matthew's gospel is the only gospel to speak explicitly of the 'church' (*ekklesia* in Greek). It contains the commissioning of Peter by Jesus (*Matthew* 16:18). The faith of Peter, which will be sorely challenged and is not without fault, is nevertheless the rock of the Church. Jesus instructs the disciples about community life (*Matthew* 18). Matthew alone includes in his gospel the presentation of the Last Judgement, a dramatic challenge to the service of the least of our brothers and sisters (*Matthew* 25:31-46). This challenge should never be forgotten by Christians, especially in our day, when so many of our brothers

and sisters are in need and suffering from poverty, sickness, oppression or violence, and when the means to remedy so many situations of want are available to the powerful. The Gospel of Matthew, which had begun with the magi from distant lands, ends with the mission to the nations. Jesus, who came first for his own Jewish people, sends out the disciples to teach the gospel to all nations and to baptise (*Matthew* 28:16-20).

53. Luke's stories of the birth of Jesus
Like the Gospel of Matthew, the Gospel of Luke also begins with stories of Jesus' birth, but in Luke they are much more extensive, providing rich and beautiful meditations on both John the Baptist and Jesus. We hear first of the annunciation and birth of the Baptist. He is born to aged parents, Elizabeth and Zechariah, but the conception of Jesus is even more wonderful. Mary is told that the Spirit of God will overshadow her. The child is conceived by the power of God. In Luke's stories of the birth of Jesus the focus is on Mary. She is the one who is 'full of grace' (*Luke* 1:28). She hears and conceives the Word of God. She is the 'servant of the Lord' (*Luke* 1:38). She proclaims the greatness of the Lord in her canticle, the *Magnificat* (*Luke* 1:46-55). The story of the birth of Jesus is set in the context of world history, with Luke's reference to contemporary rulers, including Caesar Augustus (*Luke* 2:1). Despite this universal vision, the first visitors to Jesus are local shepherds, despised and excluded in those days. Luke also shows the fidelity of Mary and Joseph to their Jewish faith in their visits to the temple in Jerusalem. Mary is a model for all in her acceptance of the will of God, which will include suffering, and her pondering of God's ways in her heart (*Luke* 2:19, 2:35, 2:51).

54. The good news to the poor
Luke states his reason for writing the gospel in his opening verses. He affirms that others have already written, but he too has traditions to record, from both eye-witnesses and preachers, to confirm the faith of his listeners (*Luke* 1:1-4). Luke, like Matthew, adapts the basic story of Mark by narrating one journey of Jesus to Jerusalem during his ministry. The ministry begins for Luke with the visit of Jesus to

Nazareth, where, by reading words from the Book of Isaiah, he proclaims the purpose of his mission: 'The Spirit of the Lord is upon me, because he has anointed me to bring good news to the poor.' (*Luke* 4:18) Jesus reaches out to the sinners, to the sick, to those who are poor, to those whom society rejects, to the foreigners. This ministry of inclusion constantly challenges Christians to reach out particularly to those who have meagre resources and to those who are despised. The good news is that all are cherished children of God.

55. The ministry of Jesus to women and their ministry to him
In his opening chapters Luke focussed on the holiness of Mary, that she above all others heard the word of God and kept it (*Luke* 11:28). Luke also stressed the faith of Elizabeth and Anna. Throughout his gospel he recounts the ministry of Jesus to women, and their ministry to him. He heals the son of the widow of Nain (*Luke* 7:11-17). The sinner woman in the house of Simon ministers to Jesus out of awareness that her sins, her many sins, have been forgiven. She is an example of the love born of forgiveness (*Luke* 7:36-50). Luke reports that certain women, among them Mary of Magdala, whom Jesus had healed of serious sickness, both accompany Jesus and provide for him (*Luke* 8:1-3). Martha ministers to Jesus, while Mary attends to his teaching (*Luke* 10:42). Women follow Jesus even on the road to Calvary (*Luke* 23:27). Luke thus stresses, as does no other evangelist, the close involvement of women in the ministry of Jesus.

56. To seek out and to save the lost
Luke inserts much new material in the narrative of the journey of Jesus to Jerusalem, including parables only found in this gospel and treasured by Christians. The good Samaritan, a member of a despised people, becomes an example of loving service (*Luke* 10:29-37). The parable of the Prodigal Son emphasises the younger son's willingness to seek forgiveness, the welcoming embrace of the loving father, and particularly the need of the righteous elder brother to imitate the forgiving welcome of the father by a change of heart in his attitude to those who fail (*Luke* 15:11-32). It is a powerful parable with much to nourish our hearts. The parable of the Rich Man and Lazarus throws

down a strong challenge to Christians to care for those in need who cry out to them (*Luke* 16:19-31). It is a parable with enormous relevance to the world of today. As Jesus reaches Jericho, he encounters Zacchaeus and proclaims the purpose of his ministry: 'The Son of Man came to seek out and to save the lost.' (*Luke* 19:10)

57. Did not our hearts burn within us?
Luke's account of the death of Jesus shows him reaching out repeatedly with healing and forgiveness. The good thief hears the words: 'Today you will be with me in paradise.' (*Luke* 23:43) The atmosphere of the story of Jesus' death is softened, as the crowds return home beating their breasts in sorrow (*Luke* 23:48), and the acquaintances of Jesus watch from a distance (*Luke* 23:49). Luke's stories of the appearances of the risen Jesus are elaborate. The encounter of Jesus with the two disciples on the road to Emmaus shows the transforming, healing power of the presence of the Risen Lord through his gifts of Scripture and Eucharist. The hearts of the disciples 'burned within them' as Jesus explained the Scriptures to them (*Luke* 24:32). Our hearts can have the same experience of Christ's presence on our journey through his gifts of word and sacrament.

58. The Fourth Gospel
While Matthew and Luke adapted Mark's outline to set down the traditions about Jesus and elaborated these with new insights about his identity and purpose, the Gospel of John has quite a different layout and reaches new heights in setting forth the fulness of Christian faith about Jesus, the Son of God. In the Prologue of the gospel Jesus is presented as the Word, who was with God in the beginning, who is God, and who became flesh and lived among us. He is the 'grace and truth' of God (*John* 1:14). From the very start of the story Jesus is acclaimed with various titles, 'Lamb of God', 'Messiah', 'Son of God', 'King of Israel'. By contrast with the synoptic gospels the disciples 'see his glory', they recognise his true identity, from the beginning (*John* 2:11).

59. The signs in John's gospel

John calls the miracles of Jesus 'signs', in order to emphasise their deeper, christological sense. The focus of John's gospel is not on the preaching of the kingdom but on the person of Jesus. Each sign has a message to convey concerning Jesus. At Cana, where the first sign is worked, Jesus provides the wine of the messianic time (*John* 2:1-12). The following chapters contain speeches of Jesus which have been used for centuries in the Church in the preparation for Easter and for Baptism: to Nicodemus Jesus speaks of rebirth by water and the Holy Spirit, and to the Samaritan woman he offers living water welling up for eternal life (*John* 3-4). Later signs in the gospel are accompanied by extensive discussion between Jesus and 'the Jews'. As in the Gospel of Matthew, these arguments owe something of their animosity to the tense relations between Jews who had become Christians and those Jews who did not accept Jesus and the claims of divinity made for him. When Jesus heals the man born blind, he declares: 'I am the light of the world.' (*John* 9:5) This is one of several 'I am' statements which are a major feature of the rich christology of this gospel. While the man born blind regains his sight, the Pharisees are portrayed as suffering from spiritual blindness (*John* 9:39-41). In similar fashion, as Jesus prepares to raise Lazarus, he declares: 'I am the resurrection and the life.' (*John* 11:25) While Jesus restores life to Lazarus, the Jews plot to kill Jesus (*John* 11:53). The negative portrayals of 'the Jews' are clearly coloured by poor relations between Jews and Christians in the first century and should never be used as a pretext for hostility towards Jews in our day (*The Jewish People* 76-78).

the Gospel of John reaches new heights

60. Jesus' farewell words

John's gospel gives us a prolonged farewell speech of Jesus (*John* 13-17). After washing his disciples' feet as an example of self-giving service, Jesus gives his new commandment of love: 'Love one another as I have loved you.' (*John* 13:34). When the disciples are bewildered about Jesus' departure he declares: 'I am the way, and the truth, and the life' (*John* 14:6). He is the vine, and his disciples are the branches

(*John* 15:1-5). He also repeatedly speaks of the coming of the Advocate, the Holy Spirit, who will always be with his disciples, reminding us of what he taught, and leading us onwards on the way of truth (*John* 14:16, 14:26, 15:26, 16:13). That Spirit has guided the Church ever since the days of Jesus. The final chapter of this extended discourse contains the prayer of Jesus, in which he intercedes for his disciples and for all those who will come to know him through their preaching. This prayer, in which Jesus prays for the unity of all believers, is a favourite text in ecumenical gatherings as we work for the full, visible unity of all the baptised.

61. John's portrayal of the death of Jesus

John portrays Jesus as serene and courageous as he faces his death. There is no agony of Jesus in Gethsemane, for it is those sent to arrest him who fall to the ground (*John* 18:6). In the trial of Jesus Pilate appears confused and bewildered, but Pilate unwittingly declares to the world the truth about Jesus when he insists that the inscription on the cross, written in Hebrew, Greek and Latin, must remain for all to see: 'Jesus of Nazareth, the King of the Jews' (*John* 19:19-22). Only this gospel reports the presence of the mother of Jesus at the cross, accompanied by the 'beloved disciple', traditionally considered to be the evangelist himself (*John* 19:25-27). Having cried out 'It is finished', Jesus 'gave up his spirit' (*John* 19:30). The water and blood from his side have been seen as symbols of Baptism and the Eucharist (*John* 19:34).

62. The Risen Lord

John tells of the encounter of the Risen Lord with Mary of Magdala, rightly celebrated in the liturgy as the first messenger of the good news of Christ's resurrection. The appearance in the upper room culminates in Thomas' declaration of full Christian faith as he proclaims 'My Lord and my God!' (*John* 20:28) In an additional chapter we read the account of Jesus' encounter with Peter and the poignant repetition of Jesus' question 'Do you love me?' (*John* 21:15-17) Like Peter, we are called to ever deeper love. That is the essence of the gospel challenge. The Gospel of John ends with Jesus' renewed invitation 'Follow me!' (*John* 21:19, 21:22)

63. The apostolic preaching

The second work written by Luke, the Acts of the Apostles, takes the story further as the good news of Jesus is preached 'in Jerusalem, in all Judea and Samaria, and to the ends of the earth' (*Acts* 1:8). The account of the dramatic power of the Holy Spirit at the feast of Pentecost announces the birth of the Church. The speech of Peter is the first of many speeches in Acts, the focus of them all being the death and resurrection of Jesus and the consequent call to faith in him. Luke describes the early community as devoting themselves 'to the apostles' teaching and fellowship, to the breaking of bread and the prayers' (*Acts* 2:42). It remains the call of Christ today that, by fidelity to the word, to the Eucharist and to prayer, we should live as a community of love reaching out in mission to the whole world. After the account of the death of the first Christian martyr, Stephen, we are introduced to Saul and his dramatic experience of the call of Christ on the road to Damascus (*Acts* 9). Saul, also known as Paul, is the 'chosen instrument' to bring the name of Christ to the nations (*Acts* 9:15). Meanwhile Peter too experiences a vision in which he learns that all peoples are to be welcomed into the Christian fold (*Acts* 10:34-35).

> a community of love reaching out in mission to the whole world

64. The journeys of Paul

Accounts of the three missionary journeys of Paul and his final journey to Rome are also found in Acts. During his second journey Paul, inspired by a vision, crosses into Europe (*Acts* 16:9-10). Paul and his companions often face persecution from the Jews and hardships of all sorts. It is Paul's mission to the Gentiles which is the main reason for Jewish opposition (*The Jewish People* 75). When hostility to him grows from the Jews of Jerusalem he appeals to the emperor and makes the hazardous sea journey to Rome. At the end of Acts the gospel message has reached Rome, capital of the empire and destined to become the heart of the universal Church.

65. Paul's mission and gospel

We gain a more direct testimony about St Paul from his letters. The genuine letters of St Paul were written long before the first written gospel and are consequently the earliest writings of the New Testament. Paul is totally convinced that he was 'set apart for the gospel of God' (*Romans* 1:1). He is called by Christ to preach 'the obedience of faith' to all the nations (*Romans* 1:5), among whom he includes the people of Rome, whom he calls 'God's beloved, called to be saints' (*Romans* 1:7). Paul is the apostle of the Gentiles, proclaiming faith in Christ 'to the Jew first and also to the Greek' (*Romans* 1:16). For Paul, Christ is the fulfilment of the law (*Romans* 3:21-22; *Galatians* 3:24-26). Christians, baptised into new life, live by the law of the Spirit (*Romans* 8:2). Later in the Letter to the Romans Paul will consider the difficult issue of God's covenant with Israel. He employs the image of an olive tree. While some branches, the Jews who have not accepted Christ, have been removed, new 'wild olive shoots', the Gentiles, have been grafted onto the olive tree of Israel (*Romans* 11:17). Those who do not accept Christ remain beloved, however, 'for the gifts and the calling of God are irrevocable' (*Romans* 11:29). Paul thus proclaims the extraordinary gift of the new life of faith that Christ has brought by his death and resurrection, but he also leaves us in no doubt that we owe the beginnings, the roots of our faith, to Abraham and his descendants (*The Jewish People* 36).

> the new life of faith that Christ has brought by his death and resurrection

66. Pastoral problems of the pauline churches

Paul, as we have seen in Romans, makes a major contribution to Christian understanding of Christ's person and work. He also addresses various problems faced by the Christian communities. In the first and second letters to the Thessalonians he reassures Christians about the resurrection of those who have died in Christ and dampens any excessive expectations of Christ's imminent return. In the Letter to Philemon Paul deals with the delicate problem of a runaway Christian slave returning to a Christian household. In the first and second letters to the Corinthians he addresses various pastoral concerns, including disunity in the community. Paul's teaching on the role of women has given rise to much debate, especially in our own time. Paul, on the one hand, encourages the ministry of women (*Romans* 16:1, *Philippians* 4:2-3) and speaks of the role of both women and men in Christian liturgical gatherings (*1 Corinthians* 11:4-5). Elsewhere in the first letter to the Corinthians we find an instruction that women should be silent at meetings (*1 Corinthians* 14:34-35). In the first letter to Timothy, sometimes considered to be the work of a disciple of Paul, scriptural justification is given for a lesser role for women (*1 Timothy* 2:12-15). Other texts deal with the relationship of husband and wife and seem to sanction a subordinate role for wives (*Colossians* 3:18, *Titus* 2:4-5). It needs to be carefully explained, particularly when this material is used in the liturgy, that such texts come from particular social and religious settings and must be read in the context of the whole of Scripture, and particularly in the light of the testimony of the gospels to Jesus' own inclusive attitudes and behaviour. The pauline texts should never be used to undermine the dignity of women. In the Letter to the Ephesians we find an inspiring presentation of the mutual relationship of self-giving love of husband and wife, which is modelled on the love of Christ for the Church (*Ephesians* 5:21-33).

67. Christ and the Church

The letters to the Colossians and to the Ephesians provide a more developed understanding of Christ and the Church. Christ is the first born of all creation, and, being the first born from the dead, he is the head of the Church (*Colossians* 1:15-20). Christ ends the division between Jew and Gentile so that all are one in the Body of Christ, the Church (*Ephesians* 3:5-6). The first and second letters to Timothy and the letter to Titus are sometimes considered to have been written by disciples of Paul. They provide useful guidance on the life of Christian communities, describing the ministries of bishops, elders and deacons, and the role of widows. These letters emphasise the need for fidelity to the Tradition.

68. The other letters

The New Testament contains other apostolic writings, in which faith in Christ is further explored (*Dei Verbum* 20). The Letter to the Hebrews is an extended sermon, which contains both teaching and encouragement. It proclaims that the Son of God came on earth as a brother to human beings (*Hebrews* 2:17). High priest of the new covenant, he offers not a ritual sacrifice but his own life as the one perfect sacrifice for sin, and opens up for us the way to God's presence (*Hebrews* 10:19-22). The Letter of James contains wise teaching which owes a great deal to Judaism. The First Letter of Peter celebrates the new birth in Christ which believers receive at Baptism. Christians are living stones built on the foundation stone which is Christ (*1 Peter* 2:4-5). We are 'a chosen race, a royal priesthood, a holy nation, God's own people' (*1 Peter* 2:9; *Exodus* 19:5-6). All believers share in the priesthood of Christ through Baptism. The Second Letter of Peter and the Letter of Jude denounce false teaching and give encouragement for the Christian life. The three letters of John have significant links with the Gospel of John, and seem to emerge from the same Christian community. The first letter proclaims again the new commandment of love and encourages unity among believers.

69. The Book of Revelation

In its final book the New Testament looks forward to the 'glorious consummation' of the Church (*Dei Verbum* 20). It should not surprise us that extraordinarily colourful visions, many disturbing, some comforting, appear in the Book of Revelation. The writer, one called John, uses the literary genre of 'apocalyptic', which we have already encountered in the Book of Daniel, in order to proclaim the final victory of God and the reward of the saints, who have been suffering persecution. The final stages of history are brought about by the work of the risen Jesus, the Lamb who was slain, and culminate in the death of the Beast, which represents the Roman Empire, considered to be the great evil of the day, and the wedding feast of the Lamb. Such symbolic language must be respected for what it is, and is not to be interpreted literally. We should not expect to discover in this book details about the end of the world, about how many will be saved and about when the end will come. The book's message for us is that the day will come when 'he will wipe every tear from their eyes' (*Revelation* 21:4). 'They will see his face, and his name will be on their foreheads. And there will be no more night; they need no light of lamp or sun, for the Lord God will be their light, and they will reign for ever and ever.' (*Revelation* 22:4-5) With the seer of the Book of Revelation we too pray for the final coming of the Lamb, the Lord Jesus (*Revelation* 22:20). We pray for God's final triumph over all the evil in the world. We trust we will be counted among the chosen ones of God. We should always keep in mind the words of Jesus: 'But about that day or hour, no one knows, neither the angels in heaven, nor the Son, but only the Father. Beware, keep alert; for you do not know when the time will come.' (*Mark* 13:32-33). The final book of the Bible, with all its strange and difficult features, fills us with profound hope in God, who is 'the Alpha and the Omega, the Beginning and the End' (*Revelation* 1:8; 21:6; 22:13).

the book fills us with profound hope in God

Part Five
Living the word of God

The word of God is still at work in you who believe. (*1 Thessalonians* 2:13)

70. The enduring relevance of the Scriptures

In its final chapter on 'Sacred Scripture in the Life of the Church' the *Dogmatic Constitution on Divine Revelation* states: 'In the sacred books the Father who is in heaven comes to meet his children with great love and speaks with them; there is such strength and power in the word of God that it becomes the sustenance and energy of the Church, and for the Church's children it provides the strength of faith, the food of the soul and the pure and eternal source of spiritual life.' (*Dei Verbum* 21) In this document we have considered the nature of this 'word of God in human language'. We have explored the Scriptures in the conviction that they still offer powerful words for today's world. Read as the heart of the living Tradition of the community of faith, these Scriptures provide guidance on countless contemporary issues: the rights and responsibilities of the human person, the value of human life from conception to death, the need to protect the created world, the search for lasting justice and peace for all peoples (*Interpretation of the Bible* IV.A.2). The gospel of Jesus in particular teaches the value of each and every person, the love with which each person is to be cherished, and the trust we should have in the God whose 'steadfast love lasts for ever' (*Psalm* 136 (135)). In our day the Scriptures are sometimes misunderstood as undermining and even stifling human freedom and growth. They are in fact the way of truth which leads to true freedom (*John* 8:32). They are often considered outdated and irrelevant. They are in fact words of life, always relevant, always new, with the power to change and renew people's lives (*Hebrews* 4:12). Above all, in the Scriptures we find not dead letters, but Christ, the eternal Word of the living God (*Catechism of the Catholic Church* 108). In the Scriptures it is Jesus, the incarnate Word, who comes to meet us, for all Sacred Scripture speaks to us of Christ (*Catechism of the Catholic Church* 134).

71. A rapidly changing society

This document is intended not only for Catholics, but for all who are drawn to the Scriptures. Our society has changed rapidly and radically over the last few decades. It has become a multi-cultural, multi-ethnic society of many beliefs and none. Core values which had remained stable for centuries have been questioned. While so many people display responsibility and generosity in their lives, for others pleasure and possessions, selfishness and power have become life's aims. Techniques of communication have brought extraordinary advantages and possibilities, but this has led to a saturation of words and a crisis in distinguishing what is true, good and lasting from what is false, deceptive and ephemeral. In the words of the prophet Amos, there is 'a famine of hearing the words of the Lord' (*Amos* 8:11). The Scriptures offer us a way which is trustworthy, a way both ancient and new. They contain the challenge of the Christian vocation. They show us how to foster communities in which each person is respected and loved. They challenge us to live in a self-giving rather than self-centred way. *Dei Verbum* repeatedly stresses that it is out of love that God speaks to people (*Dei Verbum* 2, 14, 21). This God of love invites us in the Scriptures to build communion with each other, as we experience communion 'with the Father and with his Son Jesus Christ' (*1 John* 1:3).

> *not dead letters, but Christ, the eternal Word of the living God*

72. The new evangelisation

Pope John Paul II writes: 'It is above all the work of evangelisation and catechesis which is drawing new life from attentiveness to the word of God.' (*Novo Millennio Ineunte* 39) We are called to become 'servants of the word' in order to engage in the new evangelisation which has become necessary particularly in countries such as ours, where contact with ancient Christian roots has been lost by so many (*Novo Millennio Ineunte* 40). The ministry of the word is the fundamental component of evangelisation. The Church of today must offer the gospel in ways that are appropriate to changing times, intelligible and attractive to our contemporaries (*General Directory for Catechesis* 50). Above all, it is necessary to demonstrate that the gospel message, and the life of faith which is built on it, are not simply interesting cultural and historical phenomena, but life-changing gifts which show us the true path amid the complex and difficult problems of the contemporary world.

73. Scripture and catechesis

For those who have been evangelised the Church offers various stages of catechesis. Such catechesis has Scripture as its primary source: 'Scripture provides the starting point, foundation and norm of catechetical teaching.' (*Interpretation of the Bible* IV.C.3) One of the aims of all catechesis is to initiate a person in the understanding of the word of God. Catechesis should present the persons and events involved in God's plan of revelation and point out their salvific relevance. Catechesis will naturally select those texts which are of greatest moment in Scripture, such as the Decalogue and the Sermon on the Mount. It will present the gospels in such a way as to bring about an encounter with Christ 'who provides the key to the whole biblical revelation and communicates the call of God that summons each one to respond' (*Interpretation of the Bible* IV.C.3). Provision is made for such contacts with the word of Scripture at different points in the processes of Christian catechumenate and initiation. Such celebrations of the word of God are fundamental to Christian initiation, and are valuable both for those who are approaching Baptism and for the renewal of the whole community.

74. Scripture and the liturgy

In the liturgy of the Church we are drawn into a living communion with Jesus Christ, who reveals to us the love of the Father in the Holy Spirit, allowing us to share in the life of the Holy Trinity. In the Eucharist the Church never ceases to take the bread of life and to offer it to the faithful 'from the table both of the word of God and of the Body of Christ' (*Dei Verbum* 21). From the earliest days the proclamation of the Scriptures has been an integral part of the liturgy. Christ is present both in the word which is proclaimed and in the sacrament we share. The reform of the lectionary instigated by the Second Vatican Council offers a richer provision of biblical texts. The lectionary now includes a practically complete reading of each of the four gospels so that year by year we may come to appreciate the riches of each one. The lectionary also provides texts from all parts of the Old and New Testaments. Readings from the Old Testament have become a regular feature of the Liturgy of the Word at Mass after many centuries of comparative neglect. Such an abundant provision of biblical readings offers food for prayer and reflection and guidance for our Christian lives. We should be deeply aware of the importance of the Liturgy of the Word, taking part attentively from the beginning of the celebration and well disposed to hear the word (*Introduction to the Lectionary* 48). It is in the liturgy that we encounter 'the continuing, complete and effective presentation of the word of God' (*Introduction to the Lectionary* 4).

75. Honouring the word

The word of God proclaimed during the Mass is honoured in different ways. Particular reverence is shown to the book of the gospels: it may be borne in procession by the deacon, it may be incensed, and candles may be carried to symbolise that Christ, who is heard as his gospel is proclaimed, is indeed the light of the world. The custom of hearing the gospel standing is very ancient and of abiding significance. The books used in the Liturgy of the Word should be as far as possible worthy signs of the sacred word (*Introduction to the Lectionary* 35). It is particularly important that the place of proclaiming

The Gift of Scripture

the Scriptures, the ambo, be stable and of appropriate dignity. It stands in close relationship to the altar and their belonging together should be indicated in suitable ways such as the design and material used (*Introduction to the Lectionary* 32). To assist people to hear and take in what is read the readings may be preceded and followed by appropriate periods of silence (*Introduction to the Lectionary* 28). The responsorial psalm, an 'integral part of the Liturgy of the Word', is designed to facilitate a prayerful response to the reading (*Introduction to the Lectionary* 19). The singing of the psalm may assist such a response. The 'alleluia' or verse before the gospel provides an opportunity for all the people to welcome the reading of the gospel, the climax of the Liturgy of the Word.

76. The role of the reader
Great care must be taken in the proclamation of the biblical readings. Those who read are privileged bearers of the gift of God's word to the people of God. It follows that the reading of Scripture should never be undertaken in a hasty or offhand manner. The office of reader was prized in the early church of Rome. Given the richer provision of Scripture in our days, this role has assumed a renewed importance. We commend initiatives taken by dioceses, deaneries and parishes to provide preparation for readers, and to support their ministry with continuing formation and days of recollection. Such activities ensure the reverent and intelligible proclamation of the Scriptures, so that the people of God may 'receive abundantly from the treasury of God's word' (*Introduction to the Lectionary* 45, *Code of Canon Law* 230)

77. The homily
The Ethiopian on the road from Jerusalem to Gaza said to Philip: 'How can I understand unless someone guides me?' (*Acts* 8:31) The role of the preacher, whether bishop, priest or deacon, is to assist his brothers and sisters to understand and welcome the words of Scripture. The preacher is called upon to strengthen their faith in the word, to prepare them for a fruitful reception of the sacrament and to encourage them to embrace the demands of Christian life

(*Introduction to the Lectionary* 41). The homily cannot provide a detailed explanation of all the biblical texts proclaimed. The central contribution of the texts should be set forth in order to stimulate the Christian response of individuals and communities. The depths of the text must be revealed by the preacher. He must not be content simply to moralise, to stress the obligations facing believers, or to speak of contemporary issues without shedding on them the light of the word of God. It is the preacher's privilege and duty to proclaim at all times the good news of salvation freely offered by God (*Interpretation of the Bible* IV.C.3). The preacher is above all a witness, who makes known to others the love and truth of God, which he knows in his own heart and from his own life of prayer and service (*Code of Canon Law* 767).

78. Other Liturgies of the Word

It is not only at the Eucharist that the word of God is heard. At the celebration of each sacrament suitable readings are proclaimed, for 'Christ himself is the centre and fulness of all of Scripture, as he is of the entire liturgy' (*Introduction to the Lectionary* 5). The biblical readings nourish and challenge us as well as preparing us for a fruitful reception of each sacrament. Liturgies of the Word are also celebrated apart from the celebration of the sacraments. Such is the case when, due to the absence of a priest, celebration of the Eucharist is not possible. Liturgies of the Word in such circumstances, with the possible reception of Holy Communion, maintain the contact of the community with Christ, the Word of life, and confirm the communion of the local community with the universal church. Liturgies of the Word are also celebrated to provide additional occasions for people to come together in order to receive Christ, the Word of the Father. Such celebrations, in church, in schools, in homes, or in other places where people gather, allow us to be nourished and strengthened by the gift of God's word for our daily living of the gospel.

nourished and stengthened by the gift of God's word

79. The Liturgy of the Hours

The Liturgy of the Hours, the prayer of the Church united with Christ, which has been rediscovered by so many people in recent times, is an extraordinary means of deepening our contact with the Scriptures. In particular, with its abundant use of the Psalter, the Liturgy of the Hours encourages us to turn our reading and listening to Scripture into prayer. Furthermore, the hymns and prayers of the Liturgy of the Hours are filled with the language of the Bible and with its symbolism (*Interpretation of the Bible* IV.C.1). Pope John Paul II has written about the Liturgy of the Hours in his Apostolic Letter for the beginning of the millennium, and calls all Christians to deepen their life of prayer (*Novo Millennio Ineunte* 34). In the Liturgy of the Hours education in prayer and deepening love of Scripture go hand in hand.

80. Bible reading for all

A further significant and welcome development of recent times has been the proliferation of groups of people who gather around the Bible, to read and to study, to reflect and to pray. The ancient practice of *lectio divina*, devout reading of Scripture in groups or alone, has gained extraordinary popularity. *Dei Verbum* encourages the assiduous reading of Scripture, not only for priests and religious, but also for 'all Christ's faithful people' (*Dei Verbum* 25). This encouragement has been taken up enthusiastically throughout the Church (*Interpretation of the Bible* IV.C.2). Wherever people have engaged prayerfully with the Scriptures, their faith has been deepened as a consequence. We give particular encouragement to families to nurture a love of the Bible, so that children and young people may discover the liberating challenge of God's word and come to know Christ as the way, the truth and the life (*Novo Millennio Ineunte* 39). We encourage the young people of our communities to discover in the Scriptures the call of Christ, once directed to the disciples, the challenge of vocation. Each of us can learn to listen to God's word, and discover that God speaks to our hearts as a

> God speaks to our hearts as a person speaks to a friend

person speaks to a friend. In times of suffering and sadness, when we feel lost and bewildered, the word of God offers consolation and encouragement.

81. Biblical formation and resources

In order to support, guide and promote deeper knowledge and love of the Scriptures, resources of all kinds have been produced. More than anything else, suitable editions of the Bible need to be made available, provided with introductions and explanatory notes (*Dei Verbum* 25, *Code of Canon Law* 825). We welcome recent initiatives to provide biblical resources for children in our schools, since it is important that catechetical programmes for children and students are accompanied and underpinned by suitable biblical material. We encourage those involved in the on-going religious formation of adults to provide more resources so that the word of God may become more and more accessible, more and more understood, more and more cherished. Such biblical resources may come in a variety of formats, through printed material, the media and the internet. Initiatives to provide biblical courses, particularly for readers and for those who lead Liturgies of the Word and Bible groups, are greatly to be welcomed, as is the provision of Bible-based retreats and days of prayer. We acknowledge the work done over many decades by the Catholic Biblical Association of Great Britain and encourage them in their endeavours. In assuming membership of the world-wide Catholic Biblical Federation we have clearly asserted our intention to strengthen provision for all of us to grow in understanding and love of the Scriptures.

82. Our debt to other Christians and to the Jewish people

As leaders of the Catholic Church in these lands, we are well aware of the debt that we owe to other Christians and to Jewish scholars in relation to the progress of biblical scholarship over many decades. In times when the Catholic Church was hesitant about the wisdom of modern biblical methods other scholars forged ahead fired by their passion for the word of God. The Catholic Church acknowledges with gratitude the contributions of countless scholars, men and women of many different communities, to the great work of expounding the Holy Scriptures. We are proud that in our day the Catholic Church collaborates with other scholars and offers a valuable and distinctive contribution to the continuing work of scholarship and of biblical formation. Such collaboration over recent decades has been particularly fruitful in the work of translating the Bible.

83. Common witness to the word of God
It is a particular joy to us that so many other Christians have adopted use of the Common Lectionary, which has been developed ecumenically and is based on the Roman Lectionary. That Christians from diverse congregations are hearing and receiving the same passages of Scripture on a given day is an eloquent sign of our coming together in faith and of our desire to be one. It is another sign to the world that Christ came 'to gather into one the dispersed children of God' (*John* 11:52). May our love of the word of God strengthen our communion with each other. The Book of Revelation encourages us: 'Let anyone who has an ear listen to what the Spirit is saying to the churches!' (*Revelation* 2:7, 2:11, 2:17, 2:29, 3:6, 3:13, 3:22) It is our goal and our commitment to speak increasingly with one voice as we proclaim Christ, the Word of God, to the people of our time in these lands.

84. Our final prayer
In the book of the prophet Jeremiah we find the following advice: 'Stand at the crossroads, and look, and ask for the ancient paths, where the good way lies; and walk in it, and find rest for your souls.' (*Jeremiah* 6:16) St Paul wrote to the Roman Christians: 'Whatever was written in former days was written for our instruction, so that by steadfastness and by the encouragement of the Scriptures we might have hope.' (*Romans* 15:4) The way taught us by the Scriptures and upheld by the living Tradition of the Church is indeed an ancient and reliable path, but it leads us on constantly to new demands, new challenges, new discoveries and new life. Our earnest desire is that of the Fathers of the Second Vatican Council, that 'just as the life of the Church receives increase from the constant celebration of the mystery of the Eucharist,

we proclaim Christ, the Word of God, to the people of our time so a new impulse of spiritual life may be expected from increased veneration for the word of God.' (*Dei Verbum* 26) Pope John Paul II encourages us all: 'May the Holy Bible continue to be a treasure for the Church and for every Christian: in the careful study of God's word we will daily find nourishment and strength to carry out our mission.' (*Ecclesia in Europa* 65) We pray for this grace particularly for the people of these lands. In the third millennium of Christian faith we look forward with great hope, and we make our own these words of St Bede, that venerable monk, who delighted to find Christ in the Holy Scriptures, and who so many centuries ago concluded his great historical work with this prayer:

> 'I pray you, good Jesus, that as you have graciously granted me to take in with delight the words that give knowledge of you, so you will grant me in your kindness to come at last to you, the source of all wisdom, and to stand for ever before your face.'

Documents

Divino Afflante Spiritu (Encyclical of Pope Pius XII) 1943

Sancta Mater Ecclesia (The Historical Truth of the Gospels) (Pontifical Biblical Commission) 1964

Dei Verbum (Dogmatic Constitution on Divine Revelation of the Second Vatican Council) 1965

General Introduction to the Lectionary (Congregation for the Sacraments and Divine Worship) 2nd edition 1981

Catechism of the Catholic Church 1992, revised 1997

The Interpretation of the Bible in the Church (Pontifical Biblical Commission) 1993

De tout Coeur (Address of Pope John Paul II on the Interpretation of the Bible in the Church) 1993

General Directory for Catechesis (Congregation for the Clergy) 2nd edition 1997

The Gift of Authority (Agreed Statement by the Second Anglican-Roman Catholic Commission) 1999

Novo Millennio Ineunte (Apostolic Letter of Pope John Paul II) 2001

Speaking the Truth in Love (Report of the Joint Commission for Dialogue between the Roman Catholic Church and the World Methodist Council) 2001

The Jewish People and Their Sacred Scriptures in the Christian Bible (Pontifical Biblical Commission) 2001

Ecclesia in Europa (Apostolic Exhortation of Pope John Paul II) 2003

Collections of Church documents on Scripture may be found in:

The Bible Documents. A Parish Resource (Chicago, Liturgy Training Publications) 2001

The Scripture Documents. An Anthology of Official Catholic Teachings (Collegeville, The Liturgical Press) 2002

Church documents are also accessible from the Vatican website: *www.vatican.va*